Children in Need: A Review of Family Support Work in Three Local Authorities

June Thoburn
Jennifer Wilding
Jackie Watson

Centre for Research on the Child and Family
School of Social Work
University of East Anglia, Norwich

First Published 1998

ISBN 1 900822 20 2

PREFACE AND ACKNOWLEDGEMENTS

This publication summarises a report to the Department of Health which will be published by the Stationery Office in 1999. Most research reports are the result of team work and that is especially the case with this one. The research design is that of Jane Gibbons and it was under her direction that the first round of interviews, the survey of family support services in the three areas, and the interim report were completed (Gibbons and Wilding 1995). We take this opportunity to pay tribute to Jane's flair, energy and creativity as a researcher, not only in this project but over many years. We are grateful to Melvyn Evans for the work he put in at that stage to prepare a report on family support resources in the City areas and for his later work in compiling lists of neighbourhood resources which were used in the second round of interviews.

On family support work we owe a particular debt of gratitude to Clare Mann for permission to make liberal use of her literature review on the role of the voluntary sector with children in need (Mann 1997). The particular contribution of this research report to the growing volume of literature is fourfold. Firstly, it focuses specifically on referrals where concerns are expressed about emotional maltreatment and neglect and is the largest British cohort study which provides detailed information in this area. It places this group of families in the context of others who request a practical service or support because a child or parent has a disability. At this point we would like to acknowledge the professionalism, determination and sensitivity of the research interviewers without whom the insights into the lives of these families and their views about the services they received, or failed to receive, would be far less powerful. They were Mary Baginsky, Kalwant Bhopal, Christine Bignell, Suzanne Cohen, Samantha Creighton-Gutteridge, Valerie Golding, Suzanne Hood, Sasha Josephides, Hasina Khan, Julia McKiernan, Naresh Sharma, Maria Skinner and Sara Woodward. The data from the families is all the stronger because they were interviewed on two occasions. Secondly, the sample includes the largest group yet studied in detail of families of minority ethnic origin who crossed the thresholds of UK social services departments who were referred for or sought a service because a child was 'in need' as defined by the Children Act 1989. Thirdly, the study follows earlier work by Jane Gibbons in linking children 'in need' with information about the family and community support systems available to the parents. Fourthly, the study provides detailed information on the families who were **not** offered a service as well as those who were.

Many people have made this study possible. The research was commissioned and funded by the Department of Health, and we are especially grateful to Dr. Carolyn Davies of the Research and Development Division for chairing the Advisory Group and steering us through the changes in research design and research direction. The other members of the Advisory Group were: Rosemary Arkley, Elizabeth Fradd, Jenny Gray, Anne Gross, Felicity Leenders, David Matthews, Wendy Rose, Peter Smith and Kathleen Taylor of the Department of Health: and Michael Little and Harriet Ward of the Dartington Social Research Unit. Some were there throughout whilst others moved on and were replaced, but we thank them all for their lively and informed contributions. Also on the Advisory Group were members of staff of the social services departments and health authorities of the three local authorities. Their names are not given in order to protect confidentiality, but we recognise our huge debt to them for their time and the advice given throughout the project and, through them, to the social workers and managers who gave so generously of their time.

Without the parents who talked through their sadnesses and in some cases their victories over adversity this study could not have been completed. As we tell their stories, some details have been changed in order to protect confidentiality.

In Norwich, colleagues and students on qualifying and post-qualifying courses at UEA have provided encouragement and helpful suggestions. We particularly thank Jo Connolly and Jacquie White for help with data processing; and Ann Lewis, Beth Neil and Ann Way for help with the records search and interviewing the social workers and their thoughtful analysis of the cases they discussed. Heather Cutting as research secretary remained cheerful under pressure as she carefully typed up the data and coped with numerous redrafts. Anne Borrett was a tower of strength as usual during the final stages and Mark Barton was largely responsible for the data inputting and checking. To all of these we give warmest thanks for playing their part with good humour.

In their different ways all have made a contribution to this report but the faults and omissions are ours and the opinions expressed are also ours alone and not necessarily those of the Department of Health, nor of the agencies taking part. Finally, our thanks go to our partners and families for their patience and encouragement.

June Thoburn
Jennifer Wilding
Jackie Watson
University of East Anglia

June 1998

SUMMARY

The research in context

- This report gives findings from one of several research projects commissioned by the Department of Health to provide information on the implementation of the Children Act 1989 to be summarised by Aldgate and Statham (forthcoming). It focuses on families with children under eight years of age who were referred to fifteen child and family teams of three social services departments.

- In order to better understand how thresholds into the family support and the formal child protection systems operate, the same information was collected on referrals to the same teams requesting a service and for those arriving with a 'child protection' label.

- The growing body of research and practice literature on family support services is reviewed alongside the more extensive literature on child maltreatment.

- In the first year or so after the implementation of the Children Act 1989, the emphasis in practice was on child protection, and referrals which came with the child protection label were prioritised. More recently, encouraged by the Department of Health, social work managers have found more creative ways to sift the large volume of referrals of children who may be in need, including those in need of protection, and to seek more rational ways of allocating scarce resources.

- Most of the research on family support services has focused on family centres and on family visiting services. These studies are not always clear about the threshold for those using these services.

- There is little information about the way in which families referred because of concerns about emotional maltreatment or neglect use general family support services. When referred to specialist resources provided for those referred because of child protection concerns, they are rarely differentiated as a group from those referred because of concerns about sexual or physical maltreatment.

- A second body of research which is relevant to this study is that on the importance of social and emotional **support** as a protective factor for adults, particularly mothers, at risk of developing serious mental health difficulties.

The methods used

- The study took place in two inner city areas with ethnically diverse populations and a county comprising rural and urban populations of mainly white British descent.

- In phase one, basic information on 550 families with 712 children under eight referred over a 30 week period in 1994-5 was collected on a 'monitoring form'. These data included the reasons for referral and the team managers' initial decision on the action to be taken.

- In phase two, a random sample of 180 families was identified, including 123 referred because of concerns about neglect or maltreatment (the 'neglect' group), and 57, for comparison purposes, requesting or referred for family support services (the 'service request' group).

- Interviews were successfully completed with 122 of these families (of whom 108 were interviewed again a year later).

- If parents consented, health visitors and school nurses provided data on the health and development of the children on two occasions.

- Between twelve and eighteen months after referral, interviews took place with groups of social workers and managers in each area, and with 18 of the social workers who undertook longer-term work with some of the families.

- Social services records were examined at stages 1 and 2 and data collected on the type of service provided and on significant events in the lives of the family members.

- Quantitative data were collected on family circumstances; any health or welfare issues for parents and children; the support available to the parents; the assessment and services provided by the social services department and other statutory and voluntary agencies. The Statistical Package for the Social Sciences (SPSS) was used to analyse these data.

- The qualitative data covered the opinions of the family members on their circumstances and on the services provided. Their views were also sought on the nature of parenting and any particular difficulties in parenting a child in the area in which they lived. They were asked their opinions about 'need', 'risk', 'neglect' and 'abuse'. These data were analysed with the help of the NUDIST package (Non-numerical Unstructured Data Indexing, Searching and Theorising) as were the comments of school nurses and health visitors (on the health monitoring form) and of the social workers and their managers, on the services provided for the families in the sample, and more generally to children 'in need' and likely to suffer harm, or impairment of health or development.

The families

- Seven hundred and twelve children under the age of eight from 555 families were referred to the child and families teams during the monitoring period.

- Children of minority ethnic origin appeared to be slightly over-represented in the city areas, comprising 61 per cent of the children in City 1 and 77 per cent in City 2. Data on ethnicity were unreliable for County; County families are, therefore, omitted from the analysis when ethnicity is considered.

- More than half of the referrals in each area involved a request for general support or a specific service. Thirteen per cent involved concerns about child safety or a child left alone; concerns about the possibility of other forms of neglect or of physical abuse were each recorded in 12 per cent of cases; the possibility of sexual abuse was the reason for referral in 7 per cent of cases, and emotional abuse in 5 per cent of cases. When only child protection referrals are considered, those where the main concern was about sexual or physical abuse comprised just over a third of the referrals, whilst neglect, child safety or emotional maltreatment as the main cause for concern accounted for 64 per cent. The reasons for referral often overlapped.

- The balance between child protection referrals and more general child welfare concerns was similar in the three areas despite their very different socio-demographic characteristics. However, there were significant differences between the areas in respect of the more detailed profile of child protection concerns. In City 2 fewer referrals were categorised as involving neglect or emotional abuse and there were more 'other child protection' cases, no doubt reflecting the very complex range of difficulties experienced by families in this very deprived urban area.

- When those of minority ethnic origin were compared with white children, there was a statistically significant difference between the two groups, with the black children less likely to be referred because of concerns about sexual abuse, emotional maltreatment or neglect.

- The 'intensive sample' comprised 180 'index' children randomly selected from neglect or emotional abuse referrals and from those referred for a service. (Those referred because of 'other child protection concerns' were also included in the intensive sample since, when the situation clarified, concerns tended to be about possible emotional harm or safety.) The sample was weighted towards neglect and emotional abuse cases because the focus of this study was primarily on this group of children. One hundred and twenty-three of the 180 were child safety, neglect or emotional maltreatment referrals (over 80 per cent of these referrals), and 57 families were 'request for service' cases (approximately one in five of these referrals). Interviews were completed with parents in over half of all referrals concerning neglect or emotional maltreatment, and 14 per cent of all 'requests for service' referrals. Just over half of those interviewed lived in one of the City areas and the remainder in County. There were slightly fewer service request cases in City 1 than in the other two areas, and more in the City 1 sample were referred because of concerns about neglect or child safety.

- The families referred in all three areas were almost all living in socially deprived communities, or in pockets of social deprivation within more prosperous communities. Though most could be described as coming from a 'working-class' background, some parents had been brought up in middle-class or professional families. For the white families, there was evidence in some cases of downward social mobility, sometimes associated with disability, marriage breakdown or substance abuse. Some of the refugee or immigrant families had a professional background and had left behind a more comfortable way of life on coming to this country.

- On broad indicators of social disadvantage, there were few differences between the 'neglect' and 'service request' families.

- Families in all three areas reported many family problems and their responses to a 'malaise' schedule (Robins and Rutter, 1990) indicated high levels of stress. However, levels of stress were not, on average, as high as for a cohort of families whose children were suffering, or likely to suffer, 'significant harm' (Brandon et al., forthcoming). This suggests that for most of the families referred, emotional and relationship problems had not yet reached levels at which it might be anticipated that positive change would be most difficult to achieve.

- There was a trend towards more of the 'service request' families reporting higher levels of stress than was the case for 'neglect' referrals, and towards more of those referred because of concerns about emotional maltreatment or neglect reporting financial and partner problems.

- In order to get an idea of the types of families who might be expected to need different sorts of services, a typology developed by Cleaver and Freeman (1995) considering the full range of child abuse referrals was adapted for this research to make it more relevant to family support referrals. Just over a quarter were characterised as having long-standing and multiple problems. The largest group (40 per cent of the interviewed families) had a 'single issue', the alleviation of which would be likely to result in improved well-being. One in five had short-term problems.

- More of the white families were in the 'long-standing and multiple problems' group and more of the families of minority ethnic origin were in the 'acute distress' or 'single issue' groups.

- **It was concluded from this part of the analysis that neither the reason for referral ('neglect' or 'service request') nor the different categories of maltreatment were associated with any particular cluster of family difficulties, and were thus not a reliable guide to the type of service which was most likely to be effective.**

- Twelve months after referral it was noted that some parents (mainly fathers) had moved out, and others moved in. Fewer of those interviewed had serious problems with housing, but there was still a high level of dissatisfaction about this area of their lives. The financial circumstances of 28 per cent had got worse. **Taking practical and emotional aspects of their lives together, the well-being of 31 per cent of the parents interviewed twice had improved; for 28 per cent it had got worse; and for 41 per cent there had been no change.**

- The words of the parents are used to convey their views on 'need', 'harm', 'neglect' and 'emotional abuse' as well as on the tasks of parenting in the areas in which they lived and the sorts of services they might find helpful.

- From the detailed analysis of the characteristics of the families and their responses to these questions, it was concluded that fewer than a third of the 'neglect' referrals and a very small minority of the 'service request' families came into the 'high criticism and low worth' category of families whose parenting style is likely to lead to impairment of their children's emotional, social, behavioural and educational development. Most were struggling, with varying degrees of success to protect their children from the full impact of the many stresses they were confronting.

- A proportion of the families had been inappropriately referred and others were temporarily succumbing to emotional or environmental pressures, but would have the emotional resources to meet their children's needs if appropriate short-term or episodic help is provided.

Viewed in the light of these figures, the resources needed to provide a good-enough service to the children likely to suffer most harm in neglectful and emotionally harmful families are less than might be assumed if one looks at the child protection statistics for neglect and emotional abuse **referrals**. The challenge is to provide the longer-term, comprehensive and cost-effective services which must be available to the families in which children are most likely to suffer serious harm if appropriate help to parents and children is not provided. It is also important to provide the range of short-term services which will prevent the situation deteriorating for parents who, despite their best intentions, may otherwise fail to meet the needs of their children when faced with the problems which brought them to seek help or be referred for it.

The children

- The children were not themselves interviewed but much information about them was gained from the social services department records, the health forms, and interviews with parents and social workers.

- Over 200 children were in each of the 3-4 and 5-7 age groups; 157 were aged between one and two, and 117 were aged under twelve months at the time of referral. More of the children referred in City 1 were in the youngest age group.

- Similar numbers of girls and boys were referred in all three areas.

- When the 50 per cent of 'service request' cases were omitted, those cases in which physical or sexual abuse were the main cause for concern made up just over a third of the referral sample, whilst neglect, child safety or emotional maltreatment as the main cause of concern accounted for almost two-thirds. This pattern was broadly similar across the three areas.

- In the city areas, a smaller proportion of the ethnic minority families than the white families was referred because of concerns about physical, sexual or emotional maltreatment. Differences in the **type** of maltreatment were noted for the different minority ethnic groups, with more Asian children and children of mixed race parentage referred because of concerns about neglect (including child safety); and African-Caribbean and African children more likely than Asian or white children to be referred because of less specific child protection concerns.

- Turning to the intensive interview sample, if more than one child in a family was referred, the 'index' child was the youngest in the family about whom concerns had been expressed. A quarter were only children; there were two children in 29 per cent of the families; three children in 27 per cent and four or more in 17 per cent of the families.

- More details about the type of neglect or emotional maltreatment were available only for the 180 intensive sample cases. Physical neglect was the main reason for referral of 44 per cent of this group of children; the possibility of emotional neglect was mentioned in 19 per cent of cases and emotional abuse in 11 per cent of cases.

- There were concerns about the health or development of almost half of the children in each of the 'service request' and 'neglect' cases. In this respect city and county cases were similar. In the light of available information, it appeared that 13 per cent were not 'in need' as defined by the Children Act 1989. These were families in which a concern about maltreatment, neglect or child safety proved to be without substance, or the result of a one-off event not likely to be repeated. In cases where the children did not themselves have difficulties, they were considered to be 'in need' because their health or development was **likely** to be impaired or their needs not met because of hazards in their environment, or because of problems of the parents, including difficulty in relationships between partners or with their children.

- In some of the families where the index children did not themselves have problems of health or development, there were older children in the family who did.

- The emotional and behavioural sections of the *Looking After Children* schedules (Ward, 1995) were used with the parents. The mean number of problems was under two for the children aged under three, but rose to six for those in the 3-4 and 5-7 age groups.

- Twelve months after referral the health and development of 29 per cent of the 108 children whose parents were interviewed twice was considered to have improved; 13 per cent were rated, on all the evidence available, as having lower well-being; and 17 per cent still had problems which had neither improved nor got worse. One child with a disability had died and 29 per cent of children who did not appear to have problems at stage one still did not at the 12 month stage.

- There were 308 re-referrals of these 180 children during the year. There was information about further possible maltreatment or neglect in respect of 28 per cent of the cases in the 'intensive' sample (22 per cent of those in the 'service request' group, and 30 per cent of the 'neglect' group). An initial child protection conference was held on only 11 of the 180 children, and only nine 'index' children and seven of their siblings had their names entered on the Child Protection Register at any time during the research period. Two of these were in the 'service request' group. Two of the index children and four of their siblings were still registered at the end of the year.

These findings show that the children as well as the parents in the 'service request' and the 'neglect' referral groups shared many of the same problems, and that there were concerns about possible maltreatment amongst a small minority of those referred for a family support service as well as those who arrived with a 'child protection' label.

Support available to the families

- The families varied considerably in terms of the extent to which they could call on support from family and friends at times of stress. Thirteen per cent (mostly in City 2) had not had any contact with a relative during the previous month.

- Families were asked whether they had any-one to turn to for material help, advice, help with the children, and help with private feelings. They were least likely to be able to turn to someone for material or financial help (a quarter had no-one); about one in five had no-one to turn to for help with the children, but a smaller proportion (12 per cent) had no-one they could talk to about private feelings.

- During the year the situation improved in respect of help with the children and financial help, perhaps indicating that social services' involvement had had a positive impact in these areas for some of the families.

- Around 70 per cent who had had contact with social workers said, at the second interview, that they found them helpful, and roughly 70 per cent said they found their GP, health visitor and playgroup leader helpful. Larger proportions found child-minders, day nursery and day care workers, solicitors and hospital staff helpful. Social services' staff other than the allocated social worker (including managers and under-8s workers) and police were described as 'helpful' by lower proportions and were more likely than the other professional groups to be described as 'unhelpful'.

- Although most of the families were **aware** of at least some neighbourhood resources, most did not use them, except for day care facilities. If they used them, it tended to be for relatively brief periods.

- Whilst by no means all the families lacked support, a high proportion spoke to the interviewers of their isolation and the subjective experience of loneliness at the time they came into contact with the social services department at the start of this study.

- Although there were improvements for many of them, twelve months later the extent of isolation was still considerable, especially in the city areas. Yet in all three areas the social services departments were already seeking to put into place a more comprehensive network of neighbourhood agencies. A major challenge is presented to those drawing up Children's Services Plans, not only to encourage the voluntary, neighbourhood and self-help sectors to join in the provision of family support services, but also to find ways of helping those who need them most to make use of them.

Social work and family support services

- For around one in five of the 555 families referred for a service or because of concerns about maltreatment, the initial response was either an immediate or less urgent Section 47 enquiry to ascertain whether the children might be in need of formal child protection measures. Almost a quarter were assessed for eligibility and prioritisation for receipt of a specific service, and in a further 14 per cent of cases a service was provided immediately without any further assessment than that which took place over the phone or at a single interview. In around one case in five no further action was taken, or the case was immediately referred elsewhere. In only one case in five was there a general assessment of need (including the need for protection) at this initial stage.

- Statistically significant differences were noted between the type of referral and the nature of the initial assessment. More of the physical, sexual and emotional abuse referrals were the subject of Section 47 enquiries than was the case for neglect referrals.

- Those referred because of general neglect or more specifically because of concerns about lack of supervision were more likely (42 per cent and 47 per cent respectively) to have an assessment of need. Sixty-eight per cent of those referred with a request for a service either were provided with the service without any further assessment or were assessed specifically for that service without their more general needs being assessed.

- As a consequence of the higher proportion of white families being referred because of child protection concerns, a higher proportion of white families than families of minority ethnic origin experienced a formal child protection enquiry under the provisions of Section 47 of the Children Act.

- The largest proportions of referrals were made by health professionals and family members. Parents and family members were more likely to make 'service request' referrals. However, nine of the 27 referrals in the intensive sample made by a parent living in the household and 12 of the 13 referrals made by a non-resident parent or relative concerned emotional maltreatment or neglect.

- In just over a half of the cases the referral which led to inclusion in the research sample was the first recorded referral, although some might have made one or more enquiries to the reception or customer service team and been redirected or told that no help was available in the circumstances described. In almost a quarter of cases there had been a previous child protection enquiry. A higher proportion of the County referrals were re-referrals than was the case in either City 1 or City 2. 'Service request' and 'neglect' cases were equally likely to be re-referrals.

- During the first four weeks, 37 per cent of the families referred and included in the intensive sample had no face-to-face contact with a social worker. In these cases, social work activity was confined to letter writing or telephone contact.

- By the four week stage, half of the intensive sample cases had been closed, but half of these were re-referred at some point during the twelve months. Whilst 19 per cent of cases were only re-referred once, 29 of the 86 cases closed at the four week stage were re-referred two or more times, and four were re-referred by professionals, or family members themselves requested a service six or more times.

- Only one in five of the 180 cases remained open throughout the twelve month period.

- Forty-one of the 180 cases were provided with a planned longer-term service, although in seven cases it took three or more referrals before the need for a long-term service was recognised. Thirteen per cent of the cases received a 'revolving-door' type service in that the case was opened and closed again three or more times during the year without a long-term service ever being provided. The largest proportion (40 per cent) received a short-term service, and 27 per cent were closed quickly without the provision of a service other than, in some cases, referral to another agency.

• Families referred because of concerns about emotional maltreatment or neglect received a similar pattern of service to the 'service request' families, although there was a trend towards the 'service request' families being more likely to receive a longer-term service and less likely to receive a 'revolving-door' type service. There was a trend towards emotional **abuse** referrals being amongst those receiving a longer-term service. **Physical neglect** referrals (including the inadequate supervision cases) were less likely to receive a longer-term service.

• Assessment of needs, family strengths and problems were recorded on less than half of the files, and family support plans were even less likely to be spelled out. However, a wide range of services **was provided** to these families. Services most often provided involved practical assistance, such as the provision of day care or a family aide. In those cases which received a longer-term service, the allocated social worker provided a casework service which usually combined emotional support with the co-ordination of practical help.

• Families were asked about their understanding of the 'in need' provisions of the Children Act 1989. They were rarely provided with leaflets to explain the family support provisions, and most associated the term 'in need' with the need for child protection services.

Leaving aside the generally (though not invariably) negative comments about the way in which the investigation part of the formal child protection system was handled, the 'sins' of social workers complained about by parents were mostly those of omission rather than commission. In the light of the high levels of need in these families and at a time when prioritising or 'targeting' was the order of the day, a level of dissatisfaction could be seen as inevitable, particularly amongst parents who were denied services because they were managing 'well enough' in difficult circumstances. Towards the end of our study all three authorities had enthusiastically accepted the challenge of the policy change which encouraged them to put more of their resources into helping families through the general provisions of Part III of the Children Act 1989. County had re-organised in a way which was beginning to lead to better first stage assessments, and more sensitive services to those who might be in need of protection as well as those who knew they needed a service and sought it directly or were referred by other professionals. In the two City authorities, we were told of a deterioration in the support services available, such as family centres and nurseries. This was due to cuts in resources made worse by the unanticipated requirement to meet the basic needs of substantial numbers of asylum seekers. Without knowing exactly why, families commented with regret on the deterioration in service as they lost facilities, or a case worker whom they had come to trust had to 'pass them on' to someone else because of the regrouping of social work teams. In one of the authorities, reduced numbers of social workers were intended to be compensated for by the ability to buy into the voluntary or private sector. However, some of those interviewed considered that this was not cost-effective since, after the immediate crisis was over, some families refused to be referred elsewhere and tell their story all again to someone else. It seemed inevitable that some of these would return in a worse state of mental health for parents and children.

In the concluding section we pick up on some of the suggestions made by the social workers and the families which might lead to more rational and more clearly understandable ways of deciding which of the very many children 'in need' can be provided with more comprehensive services; and how early assessments in those cases where concerns are expressed about emotional maltreatment or neglect can help judgements to be made about when the formal child protection route is needed, and when a more general assessment and family support service under the provisions of Part III of the Children Act 1989 will be more appropriate.

The parents and children 12 months later

As well as the rating of changes in well-being of the parents interviewed and of the children, an **overall** 'researcher rating' of changes in family well-being was made in respect of the 108 families interviewed twice.

- There had been an improvement in the general well-being of just over half of the families, and the well-being of almost a quarter had deteriorated. For a quarter there had either been no change, or the outcome was positive in some respects but negative in other respects.

- More of those referred because of concerns about neglect or emotional maltreatment had improved outcomes than was the case for those referred with a request for a service. The general well-being of more of the families in the 'service request' group **had deteriorated** whilst there was no change for more of the families referred because of concerns about neglect or emotional maltreatment. To some extent this is explained by the fact that, after further assessment, some of those in the 'neglect' group did not have problems which resulted in a conclusion that the child was 'in need'. The 'service request' families on the other hand were almost all families with a child 'in need', and in more of these cases either the parents or the child had a long-term disability.

- Those rated 'not in need' or as having 'short-term problems' were, not surprisingly, more likely to show overall improvement or no change.

- The well-being of over a quarter of the children living in families with 'long-term and multiple problems' deteriorated as did that of 14 per cent of the 'single issue' families. However, the well-being of none of the children in the 'acute distress' group of families deteriorated, indicating that, despite their pressures, most parents were managing to protect their children from the ill-effects of their own stress.

- There was a trend towards more of the white families showing overall improvement **or** deterioration, and more of the families of minority ethnic origin experiencing little change **or** mixed outcomes.

- Contrary to what we might have anticipated, there was no statistically significant association on any of the three outcome measures (overall family functioning; parents' well-being; and child's well-being) between outcome and the lack of support to the main parent at stage one, although the **trend** was in the direction of better outcomes for those who did have emotional support, as compared with those who reported a lack of support in their daily lives.

- A scrutiny of the relationship between service factors, family factors and outcome suggest that it is the **characteristics of the family,** rather than the nature of the service provided, which has the greatest influence on outcome for parents and children.

- **So long as thresholds for allocation to social work caseloads remain high, positive short-term outcomes which can be attributed to any particular model of intervention are likely to be few. Those allocated to social workers were those with the most serious problems and, therefore, less positive outcomes. Those provided with no service or a short-term service were assessed as having fewer problems and therefore most likely to improve or show no change without the provision of a service. It is therefore not surprising, since they were the families who had fewer problems in the first place, that more of those who were never interviewed by a social worker improved, and fewer got worse**

- However, proportionately more of the families **who expressed satisfaction** with the short or long-term service they received **did** improve in overall well-being during the 12 month period, **an indication that attempts to work in partnership with families may be justified in terms of better outcomes, as well as for reason of professional ethics and social justice.**

- No service variables **on their own** (e.g. the provision of day care) were associated with better outcomes for the family as a whole, the parents, or the children. However, **packages of services** rated by the researchers as 'good' or 'adequate' (using a protocol based on DH guidance and the inspection guidelines and taking into account parental comments), **were** associated with better outcomes for the families.

- No one **type** of service or social work method was associated with better or worse outcomes. There was no association between better or worse outcomes, and the **recording of an assessment or a family support plan.** Indeed, when the outcome for the parents is considered, those whose files did not include a recorded assessment were more likely to improve unaided or less likely to deteriorate. This is likely to be explained by the fact that those who were most likely to improve received a quick and usually minimally recorded assessment before a decision was taken that the case would be closed.

CONCLUSIONS AND IMPLICATIONS
FOR POLICY AND PRACTICE

This study was planned, and the first round of interviews completed, at a time when what has come to be known as the 'refocusing initiative' was beginning to be taken on board by social services departments and other parts of the local multi-agency teams drawing up and implementing Children's Services Plans. The three authorities in which the study took place welcomed the recommendation that they should seek to help a larger proportion of families under the provisions of the family support clauses of the Children Act 1989, and, when it was safe to do so, to divert them away from the formal child protection system.

On reflecting on this study and the conversations which have taken place about the nature of emotional maltreatment and neglect, it seems unfortunate that, amongst users of services as well as professionals, the term 'child protection' has become so linked with acts of maltreatment that it is no longer seen as an appropriate description for the whole of child welfare work. This is a particular feature of the child protection system in the UK, since in many other countries (encouraged by the UN Convention on the Rights of the Child) child protection and child welfare are synonymous. Thus child welfare or child protection services cover all those children who in the language of UNICEF and other international bodies are 'in especially difficult circumstances'. They may be street children, they may be suffering because of bullying or racism at school, they may be lacking basic amenities or have parents who are dying of HIV Aids or other chronic diseases, or they may have parents who have mental health problems. A tiny minority of these parents will not have their welfare at heart, and will seek to harm them. Others may care deeply for their children but, because of their own problems, may be inadvertently harming them or unable to meet their needs for protection. For many children in especially difficult circumstances, protection from harm is a major issue even though they may have parents who, with appropriate assistance, would be able to adequately meet their needs.

Assessment and the patterns of service provision

How then are decisions taken about which cases will be the subject of a formal child protection enquiry; which will be further assessed before a decision is taken about whether services should be made available; and which will receive a service or be told that they are not of sufficiently high priority without any more assessment than a few phone calls, and, less often, an interview with a social worker?

The conclusions from this research are similar in many respects to those of the recent SSI Inspection Reports (DH 1997d and 1998b) in that we did not see on many of the files reasoned accounts of the processes which led to the decision to channel a family down one route rather than another. In discussing this question with groups of social workers and then with the eighteen workers who provided a longer-term service to some of the families, it became clear that a proportion of them **were** basing their judgements on theories and knowledge gained during their initial and postqualifying training. Some were able easily to articulate the principles which underlay their decisions whilst others had to work hard during the interview to get back in touch with the theories which informed their everyday 'practice wisdom' based not only on research and theory but also on experience accumulated over the years.

All three authorities did have guidelines about the priority to be given in different circumstances, but there was confusion in the minds of some of the workers we interviewed about the difference between criteria for crossing the 'in need' threshold and thus being **eligible** for services, and the criteria for **prioritisation**. It was this latter set of guidelines on which workers appeared to be basing their decisions. During the research interviews with the families and the social workers questions were asked about the extent to which decisions were based on the wording of Sections 17 and 31 of the Act. It became clear that few social workers turned regularly to the legal definition particularly of the 'in need' threshold. **It was therefore not surprising that families seemed very unclear about whether they had any rights to services and thus any rights to make representations about the non-availability of services. This applied particularly to those who requested a service, or an assessment as to the type of help which might be made available and had their request refused, especially those who themselves had disabilities or whose children had disabilities.**

The second threshold, or more often the first, since few social workers appeared to differentiate between the 'in need' threshold and this one, was the decision about whether a child and family were of high enough priority be provided with services. This applied especially to services which were more expensive and in short supply, such as allocation to a social worker caseload, day care, family aide, and accommodation for the child. In all three authorities the records of the under-8s and home care workers were not usually placed on the main family file, even at the time of case closure, so it was not possible to know how the decisions about allocation of practical help in the home and day care were taken. Towards the end of the research the language of 'first stage' and 'second stage' assessments was being used, and the process formalised, but even before this it was clear that there were indeed three sorts of assessments taking place - the quick, rough and ready decision about whether to proceed further; a somewhat pragmatic assessment about whether a specific service or resource should be provided, and a more comprehensive assessment once it was decided that further services **would** be provided. This last group included assessments of children with disabilities and those which were part of the formal child protection process which broadly followed DH (1988) guidance.

These assessments led to judgements being made (either on the basis of this or subsequent referrals, and almost always in consultation with a team leader) on which of five broad patterns of service would be provided. **The first two**, and the most frequent, responses were:

- to either provide no service or to quickly refer on (accounting for just over a quarter of the cases in both the 'neglect' and the 'service request' groups);

- to provide a short-term social work service at the same time as a 'first stage' assessment of need and priority before case closure, or referral for a specific service (by far the most frequent pattern of service accounting for 40 per cent of the referrals and used with slightly more of the 'neglect' than the 'service request' families).

The service most often provided, though rarely systematically recorded in these 'no further action' or 'short-term service' cases, was a first or second stage assessment of risk, and, in a smaller proportion of cases, need. Even when it was concluded that children were not 'in need', in most cases it was appropriate that an enquiry was made as to whether, for example, a child not being collected from school indicated a one-off incident or a 'pattern'. There were examples of sensitive one-off interviews which families found helpful. However, in some cases requests for services were refused without any full discussion with the family about the extent of need, and allegations of maltreatment were insensitively handled, leaving parents anxious about possible future consequences and determined not to seek help even if they might need it.

The third, fourth and fifth types of response, which sometimes started off as an assessment of risk in the shape of a Section 47 enquiry, and sometimes as a more general assessment of need, were:

- the provision of a package of services co-ordinated by a case-accountable social worker on a **short-term** basis, usually by the worker from the assessment team;

- transfer to a caseworker in a long-term team;

- the provision of a package of services on a longer-term or episodic basis by either a member of the assessment team or an 'under 8s' or long-term team member.

Twenty per cent of families received a longer-term service, the intensity and nature of which might fluctuate, and 13 per cent a more episodic service which we termed a 'revolving-door' type service because on each occasion, after the case had been closed, the family had to find their way back into the system going yet again through the referral, assessment and allocation process often with a different set of workers.

In a minority of cases the social worker adopted a 'case management' approach, putting together and monitoring packages of services but being minimally involved with either the parents or the children. Sometimes this was at the request of the family members, but more often parents regretted that they did not see more of the social worker who they saw as potentially helpful but too distant for them to feel able to talk through personal feelings, and relationship difficulties. There was a greater risk in these 'case management' cases that the services offered, and sometimes provided, would be inappropriate, since the worker did not get sufficiently close to the parents and children to understand what was really needed or likely to be effective. In a minority of cases, this co-ordinated package of services involved the social worker linking in a planned way with those providing therapeutic services (often mental health professionals), or with neighbourhood workers who provided high levels of support. In the City areas some Asian and African-Caribbean workers had developed excellent working relationships with neighbourhood resource centre staff who worked with particular ethnic groups. In such cases the supportive and therapeutic service was provided by the neighbourhood worker, and the good relationship between them and the case accountable social worker ensured that, if changes to the services were needed, a quick response could be made.

Do families find the services helpful, and do they appear to be effective in preventing impairment or further impairment of children's health and development?

The answer to this question has to be set in the context of the very high levels of need presented daily to child and family social work assessment teams. Without the provision of a very much higher level of resources, there will inevitably be parents who are unsatisfied by the response - in other words, they are not provided with a service which would improve the quality of life for themselves and their children, and make it more possible for them to fulfil their responsibility and ensure that their children achieve, in the words of the Children Act Section 17(a) 'a reasonable standard of health or development.' It is also inevitable that some parents will be **dis**satisfied, particularly amongst those who are the subject of enquiries about whether they are responsible for emotionally harming their children or not adequately protecting them from a range of accidents and adversities, or failing to meet their emotional needs. It is in the light of the large amount of unmet need and consequent pressure on front-line social workers that our findings on satisfaction, adequacy of the service, and outcome have to be set. In drawing attention to this, we are reinforcing the points made in the Social Service Inspectors' report which listed the challenges for social services departments. These include reduced expenditure on the personal social services; changes in the responses of NHS Trusts which diminished the services available to children and families with disabilities; problems resulting from a higher rate of school exclusions, which impacted on some of these families who had older children; and the necessity to provide financial and practical support to asylum seekers with less than full financial compensation (DH 1998b : 223).

We would add to this list the extreme complexity of the practical and emotional problems of some of the families. This complexity presents a major challenge to those responsible for devising assessment processes. Neither the **reason for referral**, including whether the case is referred because of concerns of maltreatment or for a special service, nor the **type of services requested in response to the type of need identified by the referrer**, are adequate bases for a quick decision about the sort of service to be provided. Although somewhat rudimentary, our categorisation of families may be helpful to service planners:

- Those with multiple and long-term problems.

- Those in acute distress, but with strengths which might see them through if the overwhelming pressures of the moment could be alleviated.

- Those with a single issue which distorted the way in which they were able to conduct their lives.

- Those with short-term problems often of a practical nature.

- Those who, although experiencing difficulties, would be able to manage without the provision of the extra services available under the terms of the Children Act 1989.

This categorisation proved fairly robust as a means of predicting the sort of services which would be most likely to be helpful to the families. However, it is not possible to differentiate between families without obtaining information about personal, family and community, strengths and difficulties, and about interpersonal relationships between adults and between parents and children. Our findings suggest that those assessing referrals do, indeed, take on board these less tangible characteristics of family members, alongside departmental guidance about prioritisation according to type of need and extent of risk, when sifting the large volume of cases which cross the threshold. They are certainly included in guidance on first and second stage assessments which is now being produced by local authorities in order to help their front-line workers. **Consequently, the apparently pragmatic and often ill-recorded methods of sifting the very large volume of cases works reasonably well. It does not result in the provision of inappropriate services to many families who do not need them, but does not exclude from services too many families who do need them.** However, there were some very worrying cases which were referred as often as eight times before they were recognised as families in which children's health or development was being significantly impaired without the provision of services. Had help been provided at an earlier stage, harm to children's long-term well-being could have been avoided. In other words, 'false negatives', though a minority of the cases studied, proved to be more costly as well as resulting in the sort of harm to children which it would be less possible to remedy.

Turning specifically to outcomes, given the complex nature of the difficulties experienced by many of the families, it would be unrealistic to anticipate that their problems would be resolved within a 12-month timescale. **It was concluded that the characteristics of the families had a greater impact on whether or not there was improvement or deterioration during this period than the nature of the services provided. It is a particular problem for social services departments seeking to demonstrate effectiveness that, if they successfully target their services on those in greatest need, they will be less able to demonstrate that services have been effective in terms of alleviating the difficulties. If they can intervene when problems are less serious, it is more likely that a range of interventions will be seen by the families as helpful, and will be associated with more successful outcomes.**

Given the generally negative public image of social work, it is worth noting that 70 per cent of parents described their social worker as helpful, even though a larger proportion remained unsatisfied by the resources (or lack of them) which could be provided.

Implications and recommendations for policy and practice emerging from the study

The implications and recommendations for practice differ for the different sorts of families who may need a service. It is a central theme of the research that, in the face of high levels of need resulting in large numbers of parents and children being unable to make the best use of their abilities, referrals to social services departments should be more carefully and methodically sifted than has been the case. **Parents, relatives, neighbours and professionals do not make these referrals without good cause.** Even with the small number of referrals of families which were found not to have a child 'in need' or 'in need of protection', there was a *prima facie* case for a check to be made, or the family was 'needy' but managing in adverse circumstances to provide good-enough care, and able to make use of advice and information about Children Act 1989 eligibility should their circumstances change in the future.

Central government level

- The revised version of *Working Together* should, as flagged up by the recent consultation document (DH, 1998a), **give guidance on multi-agency practice** with all children 'unlikely to achieve a reasonable standard of health or development' without the provision of additional services not available through the health, education, income maintenance and housing services.

- The guidance should apply when the need arises through parental acts of commission or omission, or because of harm inflicted by others in positions of responsibility (those covered by the **formal** child protection system), and also to those likely to suffer impairment of health or development through other causes, such as bullying, racism, multiple moves resulting from homelessness, or the other sources of stress described in this report.

- More clarity is needed about the 'in need' status of children with disabilities. The clause *without the provision of a service under this Act* which is part of Sections 17a and 17b of the Children Act 1989 is not added to the clause about disability (17c). It appears difficult for social workers and other advisers to explain to families of children with the types of disabilities listed in the legislation why services are refused. Yet prioritisation is inevitable given the volume of need arising from childhood disability. Guidance from the centre prepared in consultation with parents and older children with disabilities would be helpful.

- There is a long way to go before the communication and consultation systems of agencies, and social work practice, make a reality of partnership-based service planning and practice. The Department of Health Guidance (1995) *The Challenge of Partnership* is not widely used and could usefully be relaunched alongside new guidance on assessment and on inter-agency work.

- The Department of Health leaflets explaining the Children Act (DH, 1991b) are rarely used, and most social workers appear not to know of their existence. (We did not see them in any of the waiting rooms or offices we visited). When shown the leaflets by the research interviewers, parents usually said they had not seen them and asked to keep them. Since these are available, user-friendly and still relevant, the attention of agencies and social workers should be drawn to them and front-line staff in reception and assessment teams should be encouraged to give them routinely to parents.

- Agencies should be reminded of the guidance on Part III of the Act which makes clear that they may **not** redefine the 'in need' threshold, although they may develop protocols for deciding about the priority and allocation of services for those who **do** cross the threshold. It appears from this and our parallel study of cases of 'significant harm' (Brandon et al., forthcoming) that social workers do not routinely refer to the legislation, and are unfamiliar with the 'in need' definition. They substitute for the wording of Section 17 the departmental guidance which lists priorities for the receipt of services. This may deprive families of the possibility of making representations if they are never informed about whether their child crosses the 'in need' threshold.

- The complexities of providing an appropriate, skilled and cost-effective assessment and support service to families under stress require a more highly qualified workforce than is presently available. Managers of assessment teams, senior practitioners, and social workers providing longer-term services to vulnerable children and their families should undertake additional training within the postqualifying framework. Although there were examples of very high quality practice which were commended by the parents, their accounts and our reading of records indicate that some social workers lack adequate knowledge (including legal knowledge) and assessment and casework skills to undertake work with these complex cases. Without appropriate knowledge and skills the work will be ineffective and a waste of scarce resources, and in some cases actually harmful.

Implications for local authority planners and senior managers

- If available resources are to be used to best effect, and if cases are to be made for further resources, information is needed about the sorts of families seeking assistance and therefore the volume and nature of the different services required. This will involve some way of categorising the types of families, as well as the reasons for referral. The study suggests one possible way of broadly categorising families so that management information can be obtained about the numbers who will need a longer-term service; those who need a short-term focused service; and those for whom an efficient and knowledgeable advice and referral service is appropriate.

- Guidelines on prioritisation for the more expensive services, such as day care and longer term social work, are essential in view of the volume of need. Rather than basing these guidelines on the reason for referral or on the services specifically requested, it is suggested that those in the highest priority group should be families whose **children are most likely to be most significantly harmed or their health or development impaired if a service is not provided**. It is also important to ascertain whether there are types of families who can be provided with a short-term service at an earlier stage of problem formation, who would otherwise be highly likely to succumb to stresses at a later stage, at which point the children would have been significantly harmed and much harder to help. The rates of improvement amongst the 'single issue' group of families in this study were disappointing and they tended to get a less adequate service than those in the 'long-standing and multiple problem' group. A more carefully thought out short-term service might help avoid deterioration in the well-being of some of these children and parents.

- Multi-agency children's services planning groups should identify those high need areas within their localities from which most family referrals come, and locate neighbourhood family centres within them. They should also profile their referrals to ascertain the sorts of clusters of family problems which are resulting in requests for different levels of services. From this study, families experiencing severe marital difficulties, and particularly those who are having difficulty separating without emotionally harming their children, should be an important sub-group. Parents involved in the abuse of drugs or alcohol are another. Working parties whose members are drawn from the different statutory and voluntary agencies should then devise strategies for a co-ordinated approach to these groups of families, including responses at primary, secondary, tertiary and quaternary level. A public health style approach involving education about the harm which may result would be particularly helpful - for example, in reducing the numbers of parents who are inadvertently emotionally neglectful of their children because of marital or partner problems.

- Agencies should find ways of monitoring the way in which their reception or customer service teams work and whether appropriate decisions are taken as to whether cases should be referred elsewhere without a service, or passed through to the child and family assessment teams. There should be a system for ensuring that all enquiries to the reception team are recorded on the family's file if there is one, or logged so that families, who are not provided with a service but make several enquiries, can be identified in case more sustained help is needed.

Implications for team leaders and social workers

- Assessments should be informed by the language and concepts formulated in the Children Act 1989, and Children Act terminology should be used when assessments and family support plans are recorded.

- Assessments should contain a section which reviews previous intervention, and reasons why such intervention was considered effective or ineffective. This should include the parents' view of what they found helpful or unhelpful about the services and practice methods which had been tried.

- When assessing families referred because of concerns about emotional maltreatment and neglect, the categories of emotional neglect, physical neglect, and emotional maltreatment should be used and further sub-divided along the lines suggested by Glaser and Prior (1997) or the categories used in this study. All assessments should conclude with a clear statement of the sort of behaviour which is causing concern, and the type of harm or impairment to health or development which either has been caused or is likely to be caused. An estimate of the significance of this harm or impairment, and the likelihood of it happening, is also necessary.

- The assessment should also profile the family, identify any strengths and personal difficulties as well as relationship problems. These areas should be raised either in brief or in greater depth, depending on the existence of harm or impairment, its significance, and its likelihood of recurring.

- If there is no mandate to intervene compulsorily and the family is reluctant to receive a service, the first stage assessment is likely to be a brief one. If the family is seeking help, and effective methods of helping in those particular circumstances are available, a fuller assessment will be appropriate. In cases where a child is likely to be significantly harmed, or his or her health or development significantly impaired, a more comprehensive assessment will be necessary whether or not the family is initially willing to take part.

- Transfer and case closure reports should cover the areas outlined above so that time is not wasted if a re-referral is made.

- Family members should be consulted about the timing of any transfer from a worker in the assessment team to the long-term social work team.

- Other than with very short-term interventions, the family support social worker should provide a casework relationship and act as case manager for the provision of a package of services. Packages of services which are not co-ordinated by a caseworker, who has a good relationship with the family, are least likely to be effective, and most likely to be inappropriate or provided for either too long or too short a period to be effective.

- A particularly difficult problem is posed by referrals because of concerns about physical neglect or child safety which, after phone calls and a review of the available information, are considered to need no further action. Given the numbers of such referrals, it is appropriate that case closure is the most frequent response. If a decision is taken that the family should be notified that a referral has been made, and no further action is to be taken, a letter informing the family and telling them that they may seek assistance if they wish is not helpful, and **may** be harmful. If it is considered necessary to send a letter, a specific appointment should be offered, or a date given when the social worker will visit. Without this it is not possible to tell whether the referral has had a negative impact on the family which will lead to adverse consequences for the child.

- The most important recommendation for practice stemming from an analysis of these cases is that a careful assessment should lead to an acceptance that some cases will need a longer-term casework service, and that this should be provided earlier rather than later. A major challenge to social work managers, senior practitioners and social work theorists is to find a way of providing long-term services in the context of either a casework relationship or a relationship with multi or single agency teams based in 'user-friendly' buildings. The intensity of services provided to each family will rise and fall in response to the stresses on family members. In most cases they will only be effective if a wide range of services is available and if family members are consulted about what they would find helpful. Above all, if multiple referrals and the consequent waste of time on repeated assessments are to be avoided, ways have to be found to enhance parental self-esteem in the context of a recognition that long-term support is likely to be needed.

BIBLIOGRAPHY OF REFERENCES IN FULL REPORT

Aldgate, J. and Statham, J. (forthcoming) *Research on the Implementation of the Children Act 1989*, London: HMSO.

Aldgate, J. and Tunstill, J. (1995) *Implementing Section 17 of the Children Act - The First 18 Months*, Leicester University Press, Department of Health.

Andrews, B., Brown, G. and Creasey, L. (1990) Intergenerational links between psychotic disorder in mothers and daughters, *Journal of Child Psychology and Psychiatry*, Vol.31, 7, pp.1115-1129.

Audit Commission (1994) *Seen But Not Heard: Co-ordinating Community Child Health and Social Services for Children in Need*, London: HMSO.

Baldwin, N. and Spencer, N. (1993) Deprivation and Child Abuse: Implications for Strategic Planning in Children's Services, *Children and Society*, Vol 7, No.4, pp357-375.

Barn, R., Sinclair, R. and Ferdinand, D. (1997) *Acting on principle*, London: BAAF.

Bebbington, A. and Miles, J. (1989) The Background of Children who Enter Local Authority Care, *British Journal of Social Work*, Vol 19, pp349-368.

Beck, A.T., Steer, R. and Garbin, M. (1988) Psychometric properties of the Beck Depression Inventory, *Clinical Psychology Review*, 8, pp.77-100.

Bilson, A. and Thorpe, D. (1997) A New Focus for Child Protection ?, *Professional Social Work*, July, pp8-9.

Brandon, M., Lewis, A. and Thoburn, J. (1996) The Children Act definition of 'significant harm': Interpretation in practice, *Health and Social Care in the Community*, 4 (1), pp.11-20.
Brandon, M., Lewis, A., Thoburn, J. and Way, A. (forthcoming) *Safeguarding children with the Children Act 1989*, London: HMSO.

Brown, G., Andrews, B., Harris, T., Adler, Z. and Bridge, L. (1986) Social support, self-esteem and depression, *Psychological Medicine*, Vol.16, 4, pp.813-831.

Brown, G. and Harris, J. (1978) *Social origins of depression: A study of psychiatric disorder in women*, London: Tavistock.

Browne, K., Davies, C. and Stratton, P. (eds) (1988) *Early Prediction and Prevention of Child Abuse*, Chichester: Wiley.

Burrell, B., Thompson, B. and Sexton, D. (1994) Predicting Child Abuse Potential Across Family Types *Child Abuse and Neglect*, Vol 18, No.12, pp1039-1049.

Butt, J. and Mirza, K. (1996) *Social Care and Black Communities: A review of recent research studies*, London: HMSO.

Central Council for Education and Training in Social Work (1978) *Good Enough Parenting*, London: CCETSW.

Cleaver, H. and Freeman, P. (1995) *Parental Perspectives in Cases of Suspected Child Abuse*, London: HMSO.

Colton, C.J., Korbin, J.E., Su, M. and Chow, J. (1995) Community Level Factors and Child Maltreatment, *Child Development*, Vol 66, pp1262-1276.

Claussen, A.H. and Crittenden, P.M. (1991) Physical and Psychological Maltreatment: Relations Among Types of Maltreatment, *Child Abuse and Neglect*, Vol 15, pp5-18.

Coffin, G. (1993) *Changing child care*, London: National Children's Bureau.

Dartington Social Research Unit (1995a) *Child Protection: Messages from Research*, London: HMSO.

Dartington Social Research Unit (1995b) *Matching needs and services*, Totnes: DSRU.

Department of Health (1988) *Protecting Children: A Guide for Social Workers undertaking a Comprehensive Assessment*, London: HMSO.

Department of Health (1991a) *The Children Act 1989 Regulations and Guidance*, Vol.2, London: HMSO.

Department of Health (1991b) *The Children Act and Local Authorities: A guide for parents*, London: HMSO.

Department of Health (1991c) *Working Together under the Children Act 1989*, London: HMSO.

Department of Health (1995) *Children and Young Persons on Child Protection Registers - Year ending 31 March 1994: England*, London: HMSO

Department of Health (1995) *The Challenge of Partnership in Child Protection*, London: HMSO.

Department of Health (1997a) *Social Services: Achievement and Challenge* (Cmd. 3588) London: HMSO.

Department of Health (1997b) *Children in Need - Report of an SSI National Inspection of Social Services Departments Family Support Services 1993-1995*, London: HMSO.

Department of Health (1997c) *Children and Young People on Child Protection Registers Year Ending 31 March 1997 England*, London: DH.

Department of Health (1997d) *Messages from Inspections: Child Protection Inspections 1992-96*, London: HMSO.

Department of Health (1998a) *Working Together To Safeguard Children: New government proposals for inter-agency co-operation - Consultation Paper*, London: DH.

Department of Health (1998b) *Responding to families in need: planning and decision-making in family support services*, London: HMSO.

Department of Health and Social Security (1982) *Child Abuse: A Study of Inquiry Report 1973-1981*, London: HMSO.

Department of Health and Social Security (1985) *Review of Child Care Law*, London: HMSO.

Department of Health and Welsh Office (1994) *Children Act Report 1993*, London: HMSO.

Eckenrode, J., Laird, M. and Doris, J. (1993) School performance and discipline problems among abused and neglected children, *Developmental Psychology*, 29, pp.53-62.

Egeland, B., Sroufe, A. and Erickson, M. (1983) The Developmental Consequence of Different Patterns of Maltreatment, *Child Abuse and Neglect*, Vol 7, pp459-469.

Feeney, J. and Noller, P. (1996) *Adult Attachment*, London: Sage.

Frost, N. (1997) Delivering Family Support. Issues and Themes in Service Development **in** Parton, N. (ed) *Child Protection and Family Support*, London: Routledge.

Fuller, R. (1992) *In Search of Prevention*, Aldershot: Avebury.

Garbarino, J. and Sherman, P. (1980) High Risk Neighbourhoods and High Risk Families: The Ecology of Child Maltreatment, *Child Development*, Vol 51, pp188-198

Gardner, R. (1992) *Preventive Social Work with Families*, London: National Children's Bureau.

Gibbons, J. (1990) *Family Support and Prevention: Studies in Local Areas*, London: HMSO.

Gibbons, J. (1991) Children in Need and their Families: Outcomes of Referrals to Social Services, *British Journal of Social Work*, Vol 21, pp217-227.

Gibbons, J. (ed) (1992) *The Children Act and Family Support: Principles into Practice*, London: HMSO

Gibbons, J., Conroy, S. and Bell, C. (1995) *Operating the Child Protection System*, London: HMSO.

Gibbons, J. and Wilding, J. (1995) *Needs, Risks and Family Support Plans: Social Services Departments' responses to neglected children. Interim Report to Department of Health*, Norwich: University of East Anglia.

Glaser, D. and Prior, V. (1997) Is the term child protection applicable to emotional abuse?, *Child Abuse Review*, Vol.6, pp.315-329.

Goodyer, I.M. (1990) Family Relationships, Life Events and Childhood Psychopathology, *Journal of Child Psychology and Psychiatry*, Vol 31, No.1, pp161-192.

Hall, A.S. (1974) *The Point of Entry: A study of client reception in the social services*, National Institute Social Services Library No.27, London: George Allen & Unwin.

Hardiker, P., Exton, K. and Barker, M. (1991) The Social Policy Contexts of Prevention in Child Care, *British Journal of Social Work*, Vol 21, pp341-359.

Harris, T. (1993) Surviving childhood adversity **in** Ferguson, H., Gillgan, R. and Torode, B. (eds) *Surviving childhood adversity: Issues for policy and practice*, Dublin: University of Dublin Press.

Hashima, P.Y. and Amato, P.R. (1994) Poverty, Social Support, and Parental Behaviour, *Child Development*, Vol 63, pp394-403.

Hegar, R.L. and Yungman, J.J. (1989) Towards a Causal Typology of Child Neglect, *Children and Youth Services Review*, Vol 11, pp203-220.

HMSO (1946) *Report of the Care of Children Committee* Cmd 6922 (The Curtis Committee Report).

Home Office, Department of Health, Department of Education and Science and Welsh Office (1991) *Working Together Under the Children Act 1989*, London: HMSO.

House of Commons Social Services Committee (1984) *Report of the Social Services Committee Children in Care* (The Short Report), London: HMSO.

Iwaniek, D. (1995) *The Emotionally Abused and Neglected Child: Identification, Assessment and Intervention*, Chichester: Wiley.

Iwaniek, D. (1997) Emotional Maltreatment and Failure-to-thrive, *Child Abuse Review*, Vol.6, pp.370-388.

Jones, A. and Bilton, K (1994) *The Future Shape of Children's Services*, London: National Children's Bureau.

Jones, M.A. (1985) *A Second Chance for Families - 5 Years Later*, New York: Child Welfare League of America.

Kurtz, P.D., Gaudin, J.M., Wodarski, J.S. and Howing, P.T. (1993) Maltreatment and the school-age child: school performance consequences, *Child Abuse and Neglect*, 17, 5, pp.581-589.

Lidbetter, E.J. (1993) *Heredity and the Social Problem Group Vol.1*, London: Edward Arnold and Company.

Long, G. (1995) Family Poverty and the Role of Family Support Work **in** in Hill, M., Hawthorne-Kirk, R. and Part, D. (eds) *Supporting Families*, Edinburgh: HMSO.

Macdonald, G. and Roberts, H. (1995) *What works in the early years?*, London: Barnardos.

Mann, C. (1997) *Children in Need: The Role of the Voluntary Sector*. Dissertation for the Degree of MA in Social Work (unpublished), Norwich: University of East Anglia.

Margolin, L. (1990) Fatal Child Neglect, *Child Welfare*, 69, pp.309-319.

Martin, M.J. and Waters, J. (1982) Familial Correlates of Selected Types of Child Abuse and Neglect, *Journal of Marriage and the Family*, Vol 44, pp267-276.

Moncher, F. (1995) Social Isolation and Child Abuse Risk, *Families in Society*, September, pp421-431.

Noble, M. and Smith, T. (1994) Children in Need: Using Geographical Information Systems to Inform Strategic Planning for Social Services Provision, *Children and Society*, Vol 8, No. 4, pp360-376.

O'Hagan, K. (1993) *Emotional and Psychological Abuse of Children*, Buckingham: Open University Press.

Olds, D.L., Henderson Jr, C.R., Chamberlin, R. and Tatelbaum, R. (1986) Preventing Child Abuse and Neglect: A Randomized Trial of Nurse Home Visitation, *Paediatrics*, Vol 78, pp65-78.

Parker, R.A. (ed.) (1980) *Caring for Separated Children: Plans, Procedures and Priorities*, London: Macmillan

Parton, N. (1991) *Governing the Family. Childcare, Child Protection and The State*, London: MacMillan.

Parton, N. (1995) Neglect as Child Protection: The Political Context and the Practical Outcomes, *Children and Society*, Vol 9, No. 1, pp67-89.

Philp, A.F. and Timms, N. (1957) *The Problem of the Problem Family*, Family Service Units.

Polansky, N. (1981) *Damaged Parents: An Anatomy of Child Neglect*, Chicago: University of Chicago Press.

Reder, P., Duncan, S. and Gray, M. (1993) *Beyond blame: Child abuse tragedies revisited*, London: Routledge.

Roberts, I. (1996) Family Support and the Health of Children, *Children and Society*, Vol 10, pp217-224.

Robins, L.N. and Rutter, M. (1998) *Straight and Devious Pathways from Childhood to Adulthood*, Cambridge: Cambridge University Press.

Rose, W. (1994) *An Overview of the Developments of Services - The Relationship Between Protection and Family Support and the Intentions of the Children Act 1989,* Department of Health Paper for the Sieff Conference, 5 September.

Rutter, M. (1975) Attainment and adjustment in two geographic areas, *British Journal of Psychiatry,* 125, pp.493-509

Rutter, M., Tizard, J. and Whitmore, K. (eds.) (1981) *Education, health and behaviour,* London: Longmans.

Seagull, E. A. W. (1987) Social Support and Child Maltreatment: A Review of the Evidence *Child Abuse and Neglect,* Vol 11, pp41-52.

Shaw, D.S. and Vondra, J.I. (1993) Chronic Family Adversity and Infant Attachment Security, *Journal of Child Psychology and Psychiatry,* Vol 34, No.7, pp1205-1215.

Sheppard, M. (1997) Social Work practice in child and family care. A study of maternal depression, *British Journal of Social* Work, Vol.27, pp.815-845.

Shemmings, D. (1991) *Client Access to Records,* Aldershot: Avebury

Sieff Foundation (1994) *Family Support in Protecting the Child,* Surbiton: Michael Sieff Foundation.

Sinclair, R. and Carr-Hill, R. (1997) *The categorisation of children in need,* London: National Children's Bureau.

Sinclair, R., Garnett, L. and Berridge, D. (1995) *Social Work and Assessment with Adolescents,* London: National Children's Bureau.

Smith, M. (1998) *What does research tell us?* (Paper given at cross-departmental review on provision for young children), London: Thomas Coram Research Unit.

Stevenson, O. (1996) Emotional abuse and neglect, *Child and Family Social Work,* 1, pp.13-18.

Sutton, P. (1995) *Crossing the Boundaries. A Discussion of Children's Service Plans,* London: National Children's Bureau.

Thoburn, J. (1993) The role of the local authority **in** Triseliotis, J. and Marsh, P. (eds.) *Prevention and reunification in child care,* London: Batsford.

Thoburn, J. and Bailey, S. (1996) Unpublished Report. *Inter-Agency Working in Child and Family Cases in Kensington and Chelsea: An independent evaluation of current practice,* Norwich: UEA Centre for Research on the Child and Family.

Thoburn, J., Brandon, M. and Lewis, A. (1997) Need, risk and significant harm **in** Parton, N. (ed.) *Child Protection and Family Support,* London: Routledge.

Thoburn, J., Lewis, A. and Shemmings, D. (1992) **in** Gibbons, J. (ed.) *The Children Act and Family Suppor: Principles into practice*, London: HMSO.

Thoburn, J., Lewis, A. and Shemmings, D. (1995) *Paternalism or Partnership? Family Involvement in the Child Protection Process*, London: HMSO.

Tunstill, J. (1992) Local Authority Policies on Children in Need **in** Gibbons, J. (ed.) (1992) *The Children Act and Family Support: Principles into Practice*, London: HMSO.

Tunstill, J. (1995) The Children Act and the Voluntary Child Care Sector, *Children and Society*, Vol 5, No.1, pp76-86.

Tunstill, J. (1996) Family Support: Past, Present and Future Challenges, *Child and Family Social Work*, Vol 1, pp151-158.

US Department of Health and Human Services (1988) *Study Findings: National Incidence and Prevalence of Child Abuse and Neglect*, Washington: Department of Health and Human Services.

Utting, D. (1998) *Suggestions for the UK: an overview of possible action.* Report prepared for the Cross Departmental Review on Provision for Young Children, York: Joseph Rowntree Foundation.

Utting, W. (1997) *People Like Us: The report of the review of the safeguards for Children living away from home*, London: HMSO.

Ward, H. (1995) (ed.) *Looking after children: Research into practice*, London: HMSO.

Weismann-Wind, T. and Silvern, L. (1994) Parenting and Family Stress as Mediators of the Long-Term Effects of Child Abuse, *Child Abuse and Neglect*, Vol 18, No. 5, pp439-453

White, R. (1998) The Founders' Fund Lecture, *Child Abuse Review*, Vol.7, pp.6-12.

Wilding, J. and Thoburn, J. (1997) Family support plans for neglected and emotionally maltreated children, *Child Abuse Review*, Vol.6, pp.343-356.

Wilson, H. and Herbert, G.W. (1978) *Parents and Children in the Inner City*, London: Routledge and Kegan Paul.

Wodarski, J. (1990) Maltreatment and the school-age child: major academic, socio-emotional and adaptive outcomes, *Social Work*, 35, pp.506-513.

THIS REPORT IS PUBLISHED BY

SOCIAL WORK MONOGRAPHS

**School of Social Work
University of East Anglia
Norwich, NR4 7TJ**

**For information about titles (including our
highly-regarded Law Files),
or to obtain an up-to-date checklist,
write to**

The Social Work Monographs Office
at this address,
or phone 01603 592068 or 592087